in the news™

PUBLIC SECURITY IN AN AGE OF TERRORISM

Corona Brezina

ROSEN
PUBLISHING®

New York

Published in 2009 by The Rosen Publishing Group, Inc.
29 East 21st Street, New York, NY 10010

Library of Congress Cataloging-in-Publication Data

Brezina, Corona.
Public security in an age of terrorism / Corona Brezina.—1st ed.
    p. cm.—(In the news)
Includes bibliographical references and index.
ISBN-13: 978-1-4358-5034-7 (library binding)
ISBN-13: 978-1-4358-5362-1 (pbk)
ISBN-13: 978-1-4358-5368-3 (6 pack)
1. Private security services. 2. Offenses against public safety. I. Title.
HV8290.B689 2008
363.2'3—dc22

                                                            2008012567

Manufactured in Malaysia

On the cover: Clockwise from top left: Robert A. Hawkins is caught on
surveillance camera during his 2007 attack upon the Westroads Mall in
Omaha, Nebraska; on August 31, 2005, Homeland Security Secretary
Michael Chertoff designates Hurricane Katrina an Incident of National
Significance; a football fan is checked with a hand-held metal detector
before entering the Superdome in New Orleans, Louisiana, in advance
of the 2002 Super Bowl.

contents

Securing Public Places

Every day, a vast flow of human traffic passes in and out of public places in the United States. Children go to school, young adults attend college classes, and adults head to work. People board flights on airplanes, take public transportation, and pack the roads with vehicles. They visit museums, malls, government facilities, restaurants, hospitals, and offices. They attend special events ranging from concerts and baseball games to rallies and conventions.

Americans assume—and demand—that they will be safe and secure as they go about their day-to-day affairs in public places. The government and private sector put a great deal of effort into maintaining this sense of order. Regulations and safety codes aim to prevent security violations. ("Security" generally refers to the prevention of deliberately hostile acts; "safety" refers to accident prevention. The two imperatives tend to overlap.) Law enforcement officials and security personnel constantly

Passengers wait in line at Chicago's O'Hare International Airport on August 10, 2006. A display board above their heads shows stricter security measures implemented after the exposure of a British terrorist plot.

monitor activity in public places. In case of disturbance or emergency, there are standard procedures for response.

Nevertheless, Americans can have mixed feelings about the impact of some of these security measures. There is an ongoing debate over the degree to which people should be required to sacrifice privacy, civil liberties, and convenience in the name of security.

Security in a New Millennium

On September 11, 2001, the terrorist attacks on the World Trade Center in New York City and the Pentagon near Washington, D.C., changed Americans' view of national security. Much of the attention was focused on international affairs, as many people heard of Al Qaeda and the Taliban for the first time and America retaliated abroad. In addition, people began to question the effectiveness of security policies within the United States.

How had the attackers managed to slip past the watchful eyes of the Immigration and Naturalization Service (INS) and operate within the United States in the days leading up to the attack without the authorities recognizing the warning signs? The attackers were able to obtain visas and driver's licenses, rent apartments, and open bank accounts. Some got jobs and joined gyms. They attended aviation school in the United States. When two of them were detained by the INS after returning from overseas travel, they were able to convince agents that they had to get back to their flight training. On the morning of September 11, they passed through airport security and boarded their flights without being detected or detained.

In the days following 9/11, the United States reevaluated its national security policies. Aircraft were grounded until September 13. When airports reopened, strict temporary security procedures were put into place until new standards could be established and implemented. The financial markets were closed until September 13. Across the country, security was tightened at public events, border crossings, and sites considered vulnerable to attack. Americans were in shock, and subsequent

On March 12, 2002, Homeland Security director Tom Ridge, the first leader of the new department, unveils the color-coded terrorism warning system.

false alarms kept nerves on edge.

In October 2001, several U.S. senators and news outlets received letters in the mail containing anthrax spores. Five people who came into contact with the letters died. To many Americans, this seemed to confirm that the nation was under siege by security threats on every side. The government responded quickly. A new office, the Department of Homeland Security, was established, complete with a terrorism alert system, which advised Americans of current threat conditions: low (green), high (red), or somewhere in between. A sweeping new law called the Patriot Act was enacted to strengthen the surveillance and law enforcement capabilities of the Central Intelligence Agency (CIA), Federal Bureau of Investigation (FBI), and other law enforcement and intelligence agencies. The government dramatically increased funding for security measures.

Although most Americans supported strengthening national security, the broad range of new powers granted to intelligence and law enforcement organizations made some people uneasy. There was the potential that these measures could infringe on Americans' civil liberties, such as the freedom of speech, transparency of govern-ment, and a system of checks and balances within the government. How much freedom were Americans willing to sacrifice in the name of national security? After the initial panic caused by 9/11 began to fade, lawmakers and citizens began to debate the ongoing security concerns, as well as the ramifications of increased security measures.

Taking Effective Security Measures

The increased security efforts imposed after 9/11 do not necessarily affect the daily lives of most Americans in highly visible or obvious ways. Increased electronic surveillance powers are a hotly debated issue, but most Americans are little aware of the government's efforts to combat money laundering, increase intelligence sharing, or secure the nation's ports. Other than occasional

Fans attending an October 2007 football game at Jacksonville Municipal Stadium in Florida pass through a security checkpoint.

large-scale tests, the public is not actively involved in measures to improve emergency preparedness. Ordinary Americans are most impacted by increased airline security precautions and the tightening of border security, which includes travel, entry into the country, and immigration, as well as securing the geographic borders.

Nevertheless, many public institutions—and private institutions open to the public—followed the government's example and boosted security measures post-9/11. Buildings added security staff and began monitoring people as they entered some sites. Sports stadiums and museums began limiting the size of bags that people could carry and imposed other restrictions.

Many sites increased physical security measures, such as installing metal detectors at entrances and surveillance cameras throughout the premises and surrounding property. X-ray detectors can be used to reveal the general shape of the contents of bags and boxes. Surveillance cameras are a valuable tool for both deterring crime and providing evidence when a security incident occurs. Law enforcement organizations and private security firms generally install surveillance cameras in high-traffic or high-crime areas, or in places where tight security is particularly important.

There is no one-size-fits-all formula for securing public places. Securing a large-scale gathering of thousands or even hundreds of thousands of people in a major city is a huge undertaking. Coming up with a security policy for the downtown area of a small town, on the other hand, is fairly straightforward.

Most people associate security strategies with certain high-risk sites such as courthouses and other government facilities, historical buildings, transportation hubs, sky-scrapers, financial centers, and so on. In reality, though, every place open to the public has some sort of security policy in place, no matter how basic.

The average shopper running a few errands—going to the grocery store, stopping by the bank, and buying gasoline—will encounter three different approaches to security. The bank will take strict precautions to protect against armed robbery by keeping money locked up in a vault and training tellers in how to deal with the situation. The grocery store may be the most concerned about shoplifting, and there may be security cameras at entrances and exits. The gas station probably considers both armed robbery and shoplifting possible threats, as well as the possibility of people driving away without paying. It may have cameras posted near gas pumps and a sign near the register informing customers that the cashier does not have access to large sums of money. In this way, three different businesses take security precautions that are not intrusive yet still effective.

Emergency Preparedness

In addition to routine security measures in public places, government organizations and private enterprises alike must have contingency plans in place in case of emergency. After 9/11, many experts declared that the nation was unprepared for a biological, chemical, nuclear, or radiological terrorist attack. Biological weapons could be spread by aircraft or dispersed through the ventilation system of a subway. An attack with a chemical weapon such as sarin gas could cause mass fatalities and over-whelm the health system. A radiological weapon—a "dirty bomb"—could expose nearby victims to radioactive materials. A nuclear weapon in the hands of terrorists could cause a catastrophe.

Experts warned that the next threat could come when it was least expected. And, indeed, the next major disaster for the United States was sudden and devastating, but it was not a terrorist attack. It was a natural disaster: Hurricane Katrina of 2005. The hurricane struck New Orleans and left the city swamped as its protective levees failed. It caused billions of dollars in damage, many hundreds of fatalities, and incalculable human suffering and trauma.

Even as federal and state governments work to improve disaster emergency response, it is important that local governments and businesses also take preventative measures to ensure safety and security in public places. In order to stay open, different types of businesses must comply with various codes and regulations, dealing with everything from construction to occupancy limits. Although owners may bemoan the complexity and detail of some of these laws, violations can lead to tragic results, as in the case of Chicago's E2 nightclub disaster.

On February 17, 2003, a security guard allegedly used pepper spray to break up a fight in E2, a popular venue for dance parties on the second floor of a building. The noxious spray caused panic. Hundreds of people swarmed toward the narrow staircase to the main entrance. As

A helicopter team surveys a flooded New Orleans neighborhood in the aftermath of Hurricane Katrina. Three years later, damage has yet to be cleaned up in some areas of the city.

more and more people jammed themselves into the stairwell, they began clambering over each other in an attempt to escape. The people at the bottom began gasping for breath, and some suffocated from the pressure and lack of air. Before police and firefighters could break this human logjam and relieve the intense pressure of hundreds of bodies being shoved and squeezed against each other, twenty-one people died in the crush. The tragedy was shockingly senseless and unforeseen.

Legislation and Funding

On July 24, 1998, a gunman burst into the U.S. Capitol in Washington, D.C., and tried to bypass a security checkpoint. A Capitol Police officer confronted him, and the man—later identified as Russell E. Weston Jr.—opened fire, fatally wounding the officer. Tourists and staff scattered as Weston exchanged fire with another officer. Weston disappeared into a side corridor that led to the offices of Texas House Representative Tom DeLay. There, he exchanged fire with an officer assigned to DeLay's security detail. Both men were wounded, and the officer later died. Weston was taken into custody.

The incident—the first shooting in the U.S. Capitol since 1954—raised issues about the appropriate level of security measures on Capitol Hill. The U.S. Capitol is both the workplace of America's lawmakers and a tourist attraction. The Capitol Police are charged with the difficult job of overseeing public access to one of the nation's foremost symbols of democracy, while at the same time

Members of the U.S. Capitol Police force salute the caskets of Special Agent John Gibson and Officer Jacob Chestnut in the Rotunda of the U.S. Capitol Building on July 28, 1998.

maintaining a secure environment for Congress members and staff. Even more questions arose when it surfaced that Weston was included on the Secret Service's master list of potential threats, having previously made threats against former U.S. president Bill Clinton.

Much as the Capitol Hill shooting prompted the Capitol Police to reexamine its security policies, the events of 9/11 shocked the government and ordinary Americans alike into reevaluating security measures on a nationwide scale. For lawmakers, this resulted in a flurry of activity that led to the enactment of new security legislation for a "post-9/11" world.

Public Security Policy

Within two months of the attacks, President George W. Bush signed an antiterrorism measure called the USA Patriot Act (Uniting and Strengthening America by Providing Appropriate Tools Required to Intercept and Obstruct Terrorism Act). It strengthened intelligence-gathering powers for agencies such as the Central Intelligence Agency (CIA), and it authorized expanded law enforcement tools for the Department of Justice (DOJ). Many of the surveillance measures approved under the USA Patriot Act were controversial, with opponents claiming that they unfairly targeted immigrants and violated civil liberties.

The next major overhaul was the creation of the Department of Homeland Security (DHS). Before 9/11, there were numerous different federal organizations charged with managing various aspects of domestic safety and security. Shortly after the attacks, Congress began pushing for a reorganization of these various agencies and departments coordinated under a single authority. President Bush initially resisted, claiming that it would add an unnecessary layer of government

President George W. Bush discusses homeland security at Oak Park High School in Kansas City, Missouri, on June 11, 2002. Director of Homeland Security Tom Ridge *(left)* stands by.

bureaucracy. On June 6, 2002, however, the president formally proposed the establishment of a new Department of Homeland Security.

Twenty-two agencies and departments, consisting of 180,000 federal workers, were combined into the new department. They were organized into five directorates. The Border and Transportation Security Division consisted of the U.S. Coast Guard, the Secret Service, the Transportation Security Administration, the Office for Domestic Preparedness, the Federal Law Enforcement

Training Center, the Animal and Plant Health Inspection Service, the Immigration and Customs Enforcement (made up of the U.S. Customs Service, the Immigration and Naturalization Service, and the Federal Air Marshal Service), and the U.S. Customs and Border Protection (made up of the Border Patrol, Customs Inspections, Immigration Inspections, and Agricultural Inspections). The Emergency Preparedness and Response Division consisted of the Federal Emergency Management Agency (FEMA), the National Disaster Medical System, the Domestic Emergency Support teams, the National Domestic Preparedness Office, and the Nuclear Incident Response Team. The final three divisions of the DHS were the Science and Technology Division, Information Analysis and Infrastructure Protection, and Management. The secretary of the new department was given one year to complete the restructuring.

Organizing and Funding Our Security

Since the formation of the Department of Homeland Security, most observers have given its performance mediocre reviews. The reorganization was a massive challenge that imposed a new chain of command over the preexisting agencies. At the onset, eighty-eight different congressional committees and subcommittees were given oversight of budget, legislation, and other aspects. Many of the agencies were already inefficient and unwieldy, and the restructuring did not always address their internal problems. Although one of the department's primary goals was consolidating intelligence, there are still communication failures among the agencies and between the DHS and other intelligence organizations, such as the CIA and FBI.

To further complicate the establishment of the DHS, the department—with an annual budget of more than $30 billion—was inadequately funded at the start. Also, as it was being organized, some of the agencies suffered from irresponsible spending and poor accounting.

In addition, the very definition of the duties involved in "homeland security" proved open to debate. The Department of Homeland Security devotes resources to providing disaster relief and food for the poor, for example, which are departures from its primary missions. Moreover, many agencies that are not officially part of the department—the Department of Health and Human Services, the Department of State, the Army Corps of Engineers, and dozens of others—are nonetheless involved in matters of domestic security and receive DHS funds.

How does the mission of the DHS, a federal-level organization, impact law enforcement on lower levels? And how does this affect ordinary Americans in their day-to-day lives?

On July 13, 2005, U.S. Secretary of Homeland Security Michael Chertoff announces a restructuring of the department, the first major overhaul since its establishment.

One of the major goals in establishing the new department was to strengthen communication about potential threats. In 2005, Michael Chertoff, U.S. secretary of the Department of Homeland Security, admitted that the department needed to reevaluate its priorities. One of his newly unveiled "Six Imperatives" for improvement was "Enhanced information sharing with state, local, and tribal governments, and with the private sector," as quoted by Howard Ball in *U.S. Homeland Security*. Less than two months after his announcement, Hurricane Katrina hit the coast of Louisiana and Mississippi. The inadequate response of the DHS during this crisis underscored the need for reform.

Another goal of the DHS was to support first responders—local police, firefighters, and medical personnel who would arrive first on the scene in case of an attack or disaster. In 2004, the funds for first-responder preparedness programs were finally distributed, but the money was divided using a formula based on population, not threat risk. Therefore, Alaska—a state considered unlikely to be the victim of a terrorist attack—received $92 per resident, while the more obviously high terrorism risk states like New York and California received $32 and $22 per person, respectively. These poorly distributed grants led to some questionable spending. For example, a county in North Dakota purchased more biochemical suits than it had officers on its police force. The county needed to spend the grant, so it had to buy something, even though it is extremely unlikely that it would be the victim of a chemical attack and its police force is too small in number to make use of all the suits ordered. In total, about $27 billion has been allocated to first-responder preparedness since the establishment of the DHS.

Transportation Security 3

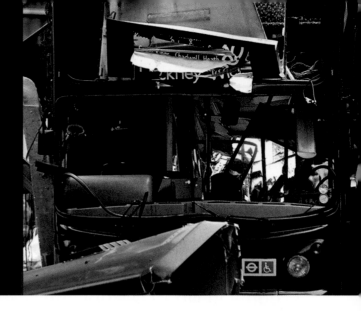

During a flight from Paris, France, to Miami, Florida, on December 22, 2001, a flight attendant received complaints from passengers of an unpleasant smell. She traced the source to a passenger named Richard Reid. He was trying to set the tongue of one of his shoes on fire, and the odor came from his sulfur matches. Passengers and crew members moved in to subdue Reid, and two doctors sedated him. The flight was diverted to Boston, Massachusetts.

Reid had been attempting to ignite a fuse in order to detonate explosives concealed in his sneakers. He had essentially turned his shoes into homemade bombs. Experts later determined that Reid's black sneakers contained plastic explosives that could have been powerful enough to blow a hole in the side of the plane, downing the flight.

The "shoe bomber" raised new fears about aviation security and the ability to anticipate potential threats. Nobody had expected an attacker to booby-trap his own shoes. Moreover, although Reid claimed association with Al Qaeda, he was a British citizen who had been born in London, England. He was a "home-grown terrorist."

Aviation Security

The aviation security system was already reeling from being caught unprepared by the attacks on the World Trade Center and the Pentagon. Rather than trying to smuggle explosives or firearms, the 9/11 terrorists relied on low-tech weapons such as

Above is the police mug shot of "shoe bomber" Richard Reid, who was sentenced to life in prison on January 30, 2003.

pepper spray and knives to gain control of the hijacked jets. Even though some of the hijackers were flagged by CAPPS—the Computer Assisted Passenger Prescreening System, intended to identify potential security threats— they were all allowed to board the planes.

In the immediate aftermath of 9/11, the government and the aviation industry moved quickly to increase aviation security and reassure Americans that it was safe to fly. Members of the National Guard patrolled airports, and military aircraft on the lookout for hijacked airplanes monitored the skies. As the initial panic abated, however, lawmakers and citizens began to debate effective long-term measures for improving aviation security. On November 19, 2001, the Aviation and Transportation Security Act (ATSA) was signed into law, establishing a security agency called the Transportation Security Administration (TSA), which eventually became part of the new Department of Homeland Security. The TSA was formed to oversee routine security procedures, such as screening passengers and luggage, and to develop long-term security strategies and programs.

Today, when a passenger prepares to travel by air, security clearance begins with a prescreening process. This involves checking that the passenger's name is not on the terrorist watch list, which includes the "No Fly" list as well as a list of individuals who require stricter security checks in order to fly. These lists are not foolproof. The terrorist watch list has been criticized for missing the names of some known terrorists due to a lack of coordination among agencies, poor planning, and other considerations. On the other hand, some innocent travelers have complained that their names ended up on the terrorist watch list in error.

The other major prescreening component is CAPPS, which analyzes ticketing information to identify potential threats. CAPPS selected ten of the 9/11 attackers when they passed through security, but screeners let them pass.

Under new measures, CAPPS selectees must now undergo a body search and have their bags thoroughly examined.

A passenger removes her shoes at an airport security checkpoint, a routine measure since Richard Reid's attempted attack employing explosives in his shoes.

Before boarding a plane, passengers must pass through checkpoints monitored by federal trained screeners. Each person must present a photo ID and walk through a metal detector. Personal possessions and carry-on bags are scanned by an X-ray machine. Due to Reid's attempt to ignite explosives in his shoes, passengers are generally required to remove their shoes and have them scanned as well. Passengers are forbidden to carry weapons or items that could be used as weapons onto a plane. In 2005, the TSA officially lifted the ban on small scissors and some small tools such as screwdrivers, an announcement that made headlines in the national news.

On August 9, 2006, police in Britain led a series of raids, arresting twenty-one people suspected of planning a terrorist attack. The authorities had been monitoring the group, made up mainly of British Muslims, since 2005. Early reports stated that the men had been planning to use liquid explosives to blow up a dozen airplanes in midair above five different cities in the United States, perhaps by smuggling the liquids aboard in sports drink bottles. The DHS responded by raising the terror alert level and restricting liquids and gels in carry-on luggage. Later on, some officials stated that the attack had not been imminent, and a few experts cast doubt on whether an attack using liquid explosives would have been likely to succeed. Nevertheless, some restrictions on liquids in carry-on luggage remain in place.

Checked baggage passes through electronic bomb-detection equipment before being loaded into the cargo hold of a plane. Screeners may also employ bomb-sniffing dogs and search luggage manually. Although baggage screening has been greatly improved since 9/11, the TSA spent about $5 billion on unreliable machinery that gave a high rate of false positive results for explosives.

Once the plane is in the air, flight crews must rely on onboard resources in case of an attempted attack or other crisis. If a passenger makes threats—or even if a passenger falls ill—the situation must be dealt with as effectively as possible until the plane has landed and the proper authorities can take over. The flight crew must be prepared for any contingency, as was tragically shown on 9/11. Aviation workers had been trained in how to act in case of a hijacking, but they had not been prepared for terrorists using planes as deadly weapons.

At the San Francisco International Airport, an officer and his dog inspect luggage, one of the heightened security measures put in place during the 2007 Independence Day holiday.

Most security situations, however, involve disruptions such as "air rage," not premeditated attacks. A passenger may lash out at a flight attendant or a fellow passenger. He or she may refuse to follow safety regulations. A passenger may become agitated or disoriented due to the stresses of air travel.

A passenger does not have to act with intentional malice in order to pose a security threat on a plane. In April 2001, Peter Buck, the usually mild-mannered guitarist for the alternative rock band REM, went berserk in the first-class cabin during a flight from Seattle, Washington, to London, England. He doused a flight attendant with a tub of yogurt while brandishing a spoon in the other hand and upended a food cart. He also insulted the captain of the plane, who tried to reason with him. Buck went to trial for being drunk on an aircraft and other charges, but the jury acquitted him based on his explanation that his behavior was due to a sleeping pill reacting with alcohol.

Behind the Scenes

Aviation security involves a layered system of security measures. One layer is intelligence—the "No Fly" list is constantly updated. If a potential attacker is somehow not listed on the "No Fly" list, he or she should be caught in one of the other security layers. The individual should be selected by CAPPS or detected during passenger screenings. Other measures include increased physical security and specialized training for screeners, flight attendants, and other aviation workers.

Another security layer is controlling access to secure areas of airports. In mid-2001, terrorists in Sri Lanka attacked the airport in the capital city of Colombo, killing seven workers and destroying half of the Sri Lankan Airlines fleet of planes. Conceivably, potential attackers in the United States could attempt to gain access to secure areas in order to sabotage aircraft or airport facilities. Therefore, the number of access points to secure areas is limited, and people and vehicles entering the airport perimeter are tightly monitored.

In addition, physical security measures aboard aircraft have been strengthened since September 2001. The 9/11 hijackers were able to gain control of the aircraft by storming the cockpit of the plane. Now, the doors to the cockpit are made of reinforced bulletproof material.

Nearly every security layer depends on the performance of the aviation workforce. After 9/11, screeners of passengers and luggage came under harsh scrutiny, as did the entire screening process and policies. The TSA quickly moved to impose higher standards, increase the number of screeners on duty, and reduce the high employee turnover rate. Implementation of these reforms proved difficult. In particular, it took longer than expected to complete criminal background checks of the new federalized screeners. There have also been cases of TSA inspectors stealing money and valuables from checked baggage. Although screening has improved, screeners have fared poorly on secret tests in which officials deliberately try to sneak weapons aboard.

The TSA developed new security protocol for flight crews that expanded guidelines on how to deal with hijackings and other security crises. There have been complaints about the adequacy of the training for crew members, however. For example, in *9/11 and the Future of Transportation Security*, R. William Johnstone notes that for teaching flight attendants self-defense, "the new system's requirements for such training can be met by an airline showing a single videotape on self-defense techniques once every thirteen months."

The TSA also assigns armed federal air marshals to some domestic and international flights as an additional security measure. They ride along anonymously, and their schedules and routes are kept secret.

In 2005, air marshals used deadly force against a passenger for the first time since the establishment of new post-9/11 guidelines. The incident occurred at Miami International Airport. Rigoberto Alpizar and his wife had boarded a plane bound for Orlando, Florida. While the plane was still at the gate, Alpizar suddenly rushed out to the boarding bridge carrying a backpack. Two federal marshals aboard chased after him, alarmed by his behavior. They claimed that Alpizar announced that he was carrying a bomb, and they ordered him to the ground. Alpizar instead began to reach inside his bag. The marshals opened fire. It was later revealed that Alpizar had bipolar disorder and that he had been unarmed. After the incident, some lawmakers claimed that the intervention proved that the new security system was effective. Some security experts, however, questioned whether the marshals' actions had been appropriate for the situation.

Violeta Castro displays a photo of her brother-in-law, Rigoberto Alpizar, and his wife. Alpizar was shot and killed by federal air marshals.

Land Transportation

Most of the TSA's focus and budget has centered on aviation security rather than land-based transportation security. Threats to aviation are perceived as more imminent and potentially catastrophic. Also, the transportation system on the ground is more difficult to protect. It encompasses about 3,995,644 miles (6,430,366 kilometers) of roads (according to the *CIA World Factbook*), as well as infrastructure such as bridges and tunnels. Railroads crisscross the nation, and many cities have bustling mass-transit systems. While airports have perimeters that can be secured, ground transportation—even urban mass-transit systems—cannot be so easily contained. The TSA has not had any major problems organizing aviation security. For ground transportation, however, the TSA has to supervise thousands of different transportation providers and authorities on national, state, and local levels.

Also, the United States has never experienced a devastating attack on land-based transportation, which makes some observers underestimate potential risks. Public transportation systems bring a high volume of people together in a small area, often with minimal security measures. Terrorists may view crowded buses or packed subway stations as attractive targets for an attack. Internationally, this has been demonstrated in recent years in attacks on mass-transit systems in Tokyo, Japan; Madrid, Spain; Moscow, Russia; and London, England.

The London bombings occurred during the morning rush hour on July 7, 2005. Three bombs exploded aboard three different subway trains at 8:50 AM. A fourth blew up an hour afterward on a double-decker bus. All four bombs had been detonated by suicide bombers. Fifty-two people were killed, as well as the four bombers, and more than seven hundred were injured. The police quickly determined the identities of the attackers—four British Muslim men ranging in age from eighteen to thirty.

After the London bombings, security was elevated for mass-transit systems in the United States. Security forces took measures such as randomly searching bags, increasing surveillance, and educating transit workers and the public about potential threats. The sense of urgency gradually died down, however, and there have been no permanent measures taken to improve mass-transit security.

On July 7, 2005, eighteen-year-old suicide bomber Hasib Hussain detonated explosives that killed thirteen passengers and mangled a London double-decker bus.

Even fewer security resources have been devoted to the nation's roadways and highway infrastructure—bridges and tunnels. Because roadway transportation infrastructure is so difficult to safeguard, security efforts have concentrated on measures such as coordinating communication between departments, assessing vulnerabilities, and emergency response planning. The destruction of a key tunnel or bridge could cause hundreds or thousands of casualties, cost billions of dollars, and severely disrupt the surrounding transportation system. In many cases, terrorists could easily accomplish this by detonating a car or truck bomb packed with explosives.

On August 1, 2007, an eight-lane highway bridge in Minnesota collapsed into the Mississippi River, killing thirteen people. Officials quickly ruled out terrorism as a cause—it was soon learned that the bridge had previously been deemed "structurally deficient" by the government. The bridge collapse highlighted the deterioration of the nation's bridges, and lawmakers pledged to devote funding to repair the tens of thousands of other "structurally deficient" bridges across the country. So far, there has not been a similar security incident involving attempted sabotage of transportation infrastructure, but the possibility remains a potential threat that has not been adequately addressed.

Everyday Security

Long before the 9/11 attacks, officials involved in national security recognized that government facilities and national symbols could become targets of terrorism or other violence. Security has always been tight at locations such as the White House, the U.S. Capitol, the Pentagon, the Statue of Liberty, and the Golden Gate Bridge. They all possess a status as national icons, and the first three of these landmarks are central to the day-to-day governing of the United States. High security is maintained at government facilities in particular in order to protect public figures such as politicians, judges, and staff members who work in those buildings.

Potential threats include domestic terrorists as well as attackers from abroad. Extremists have sometimes targeted government facilities in order to express their defiance of the federal government. The 1995 bombing of the Alfred P. Murrah Federal Building in Oklahoma City, Oklahoma—one of the most devastating terrorist

Timothy McVeigh and Terry Nichols detonated a truck bomb constructed of fuel and fertilizer in an April 19, 1995, terrorist attack on the Albert P. Murrah Federal Building in Oklahoma City, Oklahoma.

attacks ever committed on American soil—was carried out by two American citizens, Timothy McVeigh and Terry Nichols. One hundred and sixty-eight people were killed. The bombers' hatred of the U.S. government was their motive in targeting a federal building.

Public Gatherings

Well-protected sites such as government buildings, airports, and chemical facilities are known as "hard targets" for their high security. "Soft targets" are areas with low-level security that could be vulnerable to a potential attack—places such as movie theaters, restaurants, and shopping malls. Most Americans scoff at the thought of terrorists bombing a suburban mall or small-town auditorium. By contrast, in Israel—which experiences a high level of terrorist activity, including soft-target attacks—security measures such as intense surveillance and frequent checkpoints are routine.

Although it seems unlikely that there will be a surge in soft-target terror attacks in the United States, venues for large public gatherings should have security measures in place anyway in case of non-terrorist-related contingencies. In most cases, this can be accomplished by merely complying with existing safety and security regulations. In some cases, poor compliance combined with lax oversight by inspectors can prove tragic.

On February 20, 2003, an audience of four hundred people had gathered in the Station nightclub in West Warwick, Rhode Island, for a show by the hard rock band Great White. During the first song, at about 11 PM, Great White's tour manager set off pyrotechnic devices called "gerbs" at the back of the stage. The canisters emitted showers of sparks that instantly ignited the walls and ceiling of the stage. At first, many people in the crowd believed that the flames were part of the performance. Within only three minutes, the fire had engulfed the

A February 20, 2003, video image shot by a WPRI cameraman in the Station shows the crowd fleeing as fire begins to engulf the stage.

nightclub, and spectators were caught in a panicked crush for the exits. The roof caved in, trapping victims inside. In all, one hundred people died in the blaze, and more than two hundred were injured.

In the aftermath of the fire, there was a flurry of action by the authorities to revise outdated safety codes and regulations and to enact stiffer penalties for violations. The fire brought up issues of safety oversight for pyrotechnics and security issues for crowd management during crises. An investigation, however, revealed that many of the existing safety and security measures had been inadequately enforced. By law, the Station should have had a sprinkler system installed. The club owners had not installed fireproof insulation around the stage. The band's manager, Daniel Biechele, and the owners of the Station went to trial and received sentences for their roles in contributing to the disaster. A Rhode Island TV station, WPRI, also paid a fine for negligence. Ironically, the local media had turned its focus to nightclub safety and security following the recent E2 club tragedy, and WPRI had sent a crew to the Station to cover Great White's show. A cameraman had allegedly blocked an emergency exit with equipment.

Most security issues at public events are less drastic than emergencies such as the inferno at the Station. At concert and sports venues, security personnel are mainly concerned with keeping the event running smoothly. Guards are posted at key positions so they can monitor people as they arrive and keep curious spectators from trying to make their way backstage or into other off-limits areas. They are called on to stop fights, deal with disruptive or drunken audience members, and respond to reports of thefts or lost property.

Extraordinary Circumstances

For large-scale venues that hold regularly scheduled events, the security force is able to develop standard security procedures that can be adapted to most occasions. Some events are so unprecedented, massive, or particularly sensitive in terms of security, however, that they require extraordinary security measures. Large outdoor gatherings in urban areas, for example, often require street closings and involve a complex security setup, whether they're made up of spectators watching the Macy's Thanksgiving Day parade or an anti-war rally.

Appearances by public figures also call for extremely tight security. When the president of the United States travels to make a speech outside Washington, D.C., he travels with members of the Secret Service, who work together with local law enforcement officers to secure the event. Security is further complicated when controversy surrounds an event. In 2007, Mahmoud Ahmadinejad, the president of Iran, gave an inflammatory speech at Columbia University in New York City. The campus was closed to the public during the event. Tickets were sold out within the space of ninety minutes. A crowd of two thousand students, many protesting the visit, assembled outside the auditorium where Ahmadinejad spoke. New York Police Department officers, campus security guards, and members of the Secret Service assigned to Ahmadinejad coordinated the security effort.

Events such as protests and rallies require tactful handling by law enforcement authorities. On one hand, a citizen's right to freedom of expression is protected by the First Amendment of the U.S. Constitution. On the other hand, large unruly crowds can pose a threat to public safety. Organizers of such events generally need to acquire permits from the city beforehand, and they agree to a specific location and length of time for the rally.

National political conventions bring together public figures, huge crowds, and potentially contentious debates and protests. Every four years in the United States, there is a presidential election, and each political party holds a nominating convention in which delegates and fellow politicians express their support for their party's candidate. These conventions could be tempting targets for a terrorist attack. For organizers, however, the more immediate concern is how to handle the protesters that invariably turn out for the events.

The most notorious of these national political gatherings was the Democratic Convention of 1968 in Chicago, Illinois, now remembered most for the riots that occurred just outside the convention hall. The United States was then involved in the Vietnam War, and a number of different activist groups flocked to Chicago to protest the war. The city of Chicago refused to grant many of the permits the protesters requested. Demonstrators tried to march at the convention site anyway, but they were up against a force of 11,900 Chicago police officers, 7,500 army troops, 7,500 Illinois National Guardsmen, and

1,000 FBI and Secret Service agents. Protesters and police repeatedly clashed over the course of the five days. The police used clubs and tear gas against the crowds, injuring bystanders and reporters as well as demonstrators. Although the police were generally blamed for the debacle, seven political activists—the so-called Chicago 7—were put on trial for inciting riots. Five of them were convicted, but they were later acquitted on appeal.

International conferences and summits also invariably attract protesters, especially in an era where economic globalization is a pressing issue for many people. In 1999, for example, chaotic protests contributed to the collapse of the World Trade Organization (WTO) Ministerial Conference in Seattle, Washington. More than forty thousand demonstrators converged on the city. Most cooperated with the authorities, but a small number of protesters intentionally blocked streets and committed acts of vandalism. The unruly protesters and the violence of the police reaction were criticized in the aftermath of the conference.

Security in Daily Life

On December 5, 2007, holiday shoppers at the Westroads Mall in Omaha, Nebraska, were startled by the sudden sound of gunfire. The shooter, nineteen-year-old Robert

Police face demonstrators as a week of protests begins on November 29, 1999, during World Trade Organization meetings in Seattle, Washington.

A. Hawkins, had begun firing at random on a third-floor balcony of a department store. He killed eight people before ending the rampage by taking his own life. Footage from a surveillance camera later showed Hawkins entering through the front door of the store carrying what was later determined to be a semiautomatic rifle.

The tragedy dominated national news headlines for the week, but nonetheless, there was little criticism of mall security. Most Americans recognize that it's impossible for law enforcement officials to prevent every act of violence. People expect law and order in their daily lives, but they want this accomplished through minimally intrusive security measures.

Many people give little thought to the security measures around them as they go about their day. They may have to enter security codes to access some areas of their workplace or wear photo ID name tags. They may drive past a police station or walk past security guards, giving little thought to the hard, delicate, and dangerous work these people do in order to maintain public order. Some types of workplaces take extra security measures as a precaution against being targeted by extremist groups. Abortion clinics, for example, are often denounced or picketed by antiabortion activists, some of whom have bombed and shot at facilities, resulting in the deaths of several abortion clinic staff members, including doctors. Security workers must preserve the safety of clinic workers while allowing protesters to exercise their right to free speech.

Although there is a great deal of debate about the appropriate level of security for public places, most Americans agree on one point: their children's schools should be safe and secure learning environments. News stories of school massacres, in which young lives are cut short, provoke universal horror and grief among Americans. Two of the most devastating attacks were the Columbine massacre of 1999, in which two Colorado teenagers gunned down twelve students and a teacher in their school, and the 2007 Virginia Tech massacre, in which a gunman shot and killed thirty people. Statistically, very few children are killed or wounded in episodes of school violence every year, but the psychological effect of national media coverage extends beyond the physical damage.

Schools focus on implementing prevention and response measures that address a wide variety of potential security threats. School shootings are given considerable media attention, but likelier threats in most schools include gang activity, possession of weapons, theft, vandalism, fighting and other violence, drug activity, and bullying. Many schools have instituted standard security measures such as security patrols, video security cameras, and metal detectors at entrances. In addition, some schools have developed programs that educate students about how they can help create a safe and secure environment in their schools.

Myths and Facts

Myth: Public security is mainly about the blanketing of our public spaces with high-tech surveillance and detection equipment, like cameras, biometric screeners, radiological detectors, and telephone and Internet eavesdropping devices.

Fact: The frontline of public security is the funding for and training of first responders—the police officers, firefighters, and emergency response and medical personnel who are the first on the scene when trouble occurs.

Myth: Public security is only concerned with terrorism prevention or response.

Fact: Public security encompasses a wide range of activities designed to keep citizens safe, including crime prevention, disaster response, search and rescue missions, and security services at major sporting events and other large gatherings.

Myth: "Homeland Security" is a new concept, born in the wake of 9/11.

Fact: From the colonial-era Sons of Liberty and the Minutemen to the CIA, FBI, National Guard, Coast Guard, Immigration and Customs Enforcement, and Federal Emergency Management Agency, the United States has long protected its borders, gathered intelligence, and sought to identify and counter threats to the security of its citizens, institutions, and infrastructure.

The Debate Continues

What does the future hold for security in public places? Most likely, security measures will continue to grow tighter and broader in scope. More places have instituted metal detectors at entrances and other airport-level forms of security. People are watched by security guards and police officers as they go about their daily routines. Often, they may not even realize that they are being observed. Surveillance cameras connected to closed-circuit television (CCTV) networks can be used to monitor activity in an area and, according to supporters, help deter crime.

In Britain, terrorist activity by the Irish Republican Army (IRA) in the 1970s and 1980s prompted sweeping security measures by the authorities, including extensive surveillance. Around central London, the surveillance blanket is so complete that the area is known as the "ring of steel." CCTV technology is capable of identifying unattended packages and reading license plates on cars.

Cars line up for the E-ZPass lane as they enter the New Jersey Turnpike. An electronic tag on a car's windshield automatically deducts tolls from a customer's account.

New York City has begun installing a similar surveillance system in lower Manhattan.

In addition to direct surveillance measures, various databases monitor many transactions that people perform during their daily activities. Car rentals and airplane ticket purchases are recorded. Some mass-transit systems give riders the option of registering their transit cards so that when they use that card, their point of entry is noted electronically. Similarly, some commuters who regularly use toll roads buy passes that allow fares to be automatically deducted from their account when they drive past a scanner. Their entries and exits from the toll road are entered into a database. Some shoppers sign up for "preferred customer" programs at stores in order to qualify for special sales and other promotions. These stores track customers' purchases when they use their account, even when they pay by cash. Credit card companies keep records of transaction details. So do libraries.

Given access to the data from these various databases, an agent—or, conceivably, criminals or terrorists—could reconstruct an individual's movements and personal habits. For this reason, information security is intertwined with public security measures.

The Debate Over National ID Cards

For years, beginning long before 9/11, there has been disagreement over whether the United States should establish a national ID program. Today, most people carry state driver's licenses or other forms of identification, which may vary from one state to the next. Supporters of a national ID program claim that the uniform standards for issuing the cards would prevent people from using fraud to obtain IDs. Opponents counter that national ID cards would not prevent terrorism or criminal acts and, since the system would consolidate personal information, would be a violation of citizens' privacy.

In 2005, Congress passed an emergency bill on defense, fighting terror, and tsunami relief that contained a division called the Real ID Act. The act requires states to meet new standards set by the Department of Homeland Security in issuing driver's licenses. Applicants will have to present certain identity papers when applying for licenses. States will have to include certain information on the Real ID license, including machine-readable technology—essentially a bar code.

The DHS states that the Real ID Act is not a national ID system, but privacy advocates claim that it sets precedents that could lead to the establishment of a national monitoring system. Many states also oppose the bill, which would be costly to implement and potentially create bureaucratic and administrative difficulties for state governments and individuals. As of 2008, seventeen states had passed legislation opposing the Real ID Act. The DHS retaliated by threatening to ban people carrying non-compliant licenses from using them for federal purposes when the new standards go into effect. People from non-compliant states would have to show passports for boarding planes and entering federal facilities.

Biometric Screening

Some proposed security initiatives have recommended using biometrics as an additional security measure in airports and other high-risk areas. Biometric identifiers are the physical characteristics—traits such as fingerprints, facial features, voice patterns, eye retinas, and irises—that are unique to each individual. Driver's licenses contain some basic biometric information, such as hair color, eye color, and weight, but people can easily dye their hair, use colored contact lenses, and change or disguise their apparent weight.

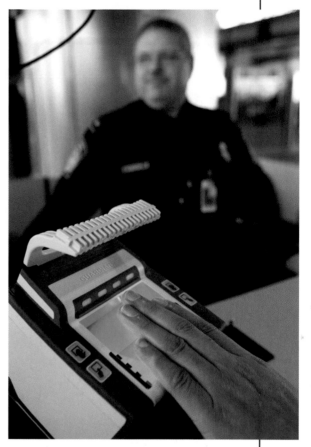

On February 1, 2008, a U.S. Customs and Border Protection officer at a Texas airport looks on as a passenger uses a new biometric system that scans all ten fingers.

In theory, biometric screening at checkpoints could positively confirm a person's identity using more specific biometric identifiers. A machine could take an image of a person's face, scan a retina, or check a finger-print. The possibilities of biometrics raise many of the same privacy concerns as national ID cards and blanket surveillance. Biometric screening is not likely to become widespread in the near future, however. Early tests show that biometric recognition technology is still unreliable.

Also, installing a biometric screening system would be expensive and complex, requiring scanning hardware, software for translating the images, and establishment of an information database.

Access to Firearms

After 9/11, some individuals and groups urged Congress to authorize pilots to carry firearms. Supporters of this plan claimed that if they were armed, pilots could potentially thwart hijackers trying to seize a plane. Opponents took the position that the pilot's job was to control the plane and that the DHS was responsible for security measures.

As with other security matters, the debate over possessing and carrying firearms extends beyond aviation security. Following school shootings, for example, state governments often review gun laws, sometimes enacting changes such as requiring more thorough background checks for prospective gun buyers. Nonetheless, there is fundamental disagreement on gun control policy in the United States. At one extreme, some supporters of gun control laws believe that some weapons should be banned and that gun purchases should be tightly regulated. At the other, gun owners contend that bearing arms is a constitutionally protected right and that responsible gun ownership is more likely to deter crime than gun control laws. The various gun laws of individual states reflect this disagreement—in some states, residents can obtain a permit to carry concealed weapons in public places.

Securing the Future

The 9/11 terrorist attacks highlighted, among other lapses, failures in intelligence, border security, and aviation security. Much of the post-9/11 media coverage focused on government efforts to pinpoint and remedy the mistakes in these areas. The government responded quickly, passing the USA Patriot Act and the Aviation and Transportation Security Act, establishing the Department of Homeland Security. Since the attacks, lawmakers and other government officials have had time to reevaluate and refine these initial reactions. If there is ever another large-scale attack, the nation will likely have to reconsider its security priorities once again.

In November 2002, Congress and the president established the National Commission on Terrorist Attacks upon the United States—generally called the 9/11 Commission—to investigate the attacks and recommend further safeguards. The 9/11 Commission members submitted their final report to Congress in September 2004.

The 9/11 Commission Report was released on July 22, 2004. It neared the top of many national bestseller lists.

Its key recommendations ranged from antiterrorism measures to specific security proposals and government reorganization.

One of the recommendations emphasized the importance of safeguarding individual privacy. Another addressed the importance of preserving civil liberties. The future may hold the possibility of future attacks and other catastrophes, and public security measures will continue to grow more powerful and common, a part of our everyday lives we scarcely notice anymore and take for granted. Still, there will always be concerned citizens, organizations, elements of the government, and even official committees such as the 9/11 Commission that will continue to champion privacy and civil liberties. They will all work together to ensure that increased security measures preserve these essential, protected American values and freedoms.

Glossary

anthrax An infectious, often fatal disease that affects animals and humans.

aviation The operation of aircraft.

bipolar disorder A psychiatric disorder marked by alternating episodes of mania and depression.

cockpit The compartment in the front of an aircraft that contains controls, instruments, and seats for the pilot and other flight crew members.

detonate To explode or cause to explode.

infrastructure The fundamental facilities, services, and installations serving a country, city, or area.

levee An embankment designed to prevent flooding.

massacre The cruel and unnecessary killing of a large number of people.

overhaul To make extensive repairs or revisions on.

personnel The people employed at an organization or place of work.

radiological Involving radioactive substances.

sarin A poisonous liquid that is used as a nerve gas.

screen To examine systematically.

surveillance Close observation.

visa An official authorization made in a passport that permits the holder to enter and travel within the country issuing the authorization.

For More Information

American Civil Liberties Union (ACLU)
125 Broad Street, 18th Floor
New York, NY 10004
(212) 549-2500
Web site: http://www.aclu.org
The ACLU is a national organization devoted to preserving
    civil liberties guaranteed to Americans in the
    Constitution.

Central Intelligence Agency (CIA)
Office of Public Affairs
Washington, DC 20505
(703) 482-0623
Web site: http://www.cia.gov
The CIA is the national agency charged with conducting
    the intelligence activities of the United States.

Department of Homeland Security (DHS)
Washington, DC 20528
Web site: http://www.dhs.gov
The DHS consists of twenty-two agencies and depart-
    ments joined by a mission of preserving domestic
    security.

Royal Canadian Mounted Police—Gendarmerie Royale
    du Canada
Public Affairs and Communications Services
Headquarters Building
1200 Vanier Parkway
Ottawa, ON K1A 0R2
Canada
(613) 993-7267
Web site: http://www.rcmp-grc.gc.ca
Canada's national police force, the RCMP, is also
    involved with criminal intelligence.

Web Sites

Due to the changing nature of Internet links, Rosen
Publishing has developed an online list of Web sites
related to the subject of this book. This site is updated
regularly. Please use this link to access this list:

http://www.rosenlinks.com/itn/psat

For Further Reading

Gottfried, Ted. *Homeland Security Versus Constitutional Rights.* Brookfield, CN: Twenty-First Century Books, 2003.

Halberstam, David. *Firehouse.* New York, NY: Hyperion, 2002.

Haynes, Charles C., et al. *First Freedoms: A Documentary History of First Amendment Rights in America.* New York, NY: Oxford University Press, 2006.

Jacobson, Side, and Ernie Colón. *The 9/11 Report: A Graphic Adaptation.* New York, NY: Hill and Wang, 2006.

Ledlow, Gerald R., et al., eds. *Community Preparedness and Response to Terrorism.* Westport, CN: Praeger, 2005.

Lerner, K. Lee, et al., eds. *Immigration and Multiculturalism: Essential Primary Sources.* New York, NY: Thomson Gale, 2006.

Maddex, Robert L. *The U.S. Constitution A to Z.* Washington, DC: CQ Press, 2002.

Bibliography

Alexander, Keith L. "Shooting Is Defended But Gets Mixed Reviews." *Washington Post*, December 8, 2005. Retrieved February 2008 (http://www.washingtonpost.com/wp-dyn/content/article/2005/12/07/AR2005120702565.html).

Ball, Howard. *U.S. Homeland Security: A Reference Handbook*. Santa Barbara, CA: ABC-CLIO, Inc., 2005.

Belluck, Pam. "Threats and Responses: The Bomb Plot; Unrepentant Shoe Bomber Is Given a Life Sentence for Trying to Blow Up Jet." *New York Times*, January 31, 2003. Retrieved February 2008 (http://query.nytimes.com/gst/fullpage.html?res=9403E2D61638F932A05752C0A9659C8B63).

Campbell, Geoffrey. *A Vulnerable America: An Overview of National Security*. Farmington Hills, MI: Lucent Books, 2004.

Ervin, Clark Kent. *Open Target: Where America Is Vulnerable to Attack*. New York, NY: Palgrave Macmillan, 2006.

Fineman, Howard, and Karen Breslau. "Slipping Past Security." *Newsweek*, August 3, 1998. Retrieved February 2008 (http://www.washingtonpost.com/wp-srv/newsweek/capitolshooting/slipping.htm).

Johnstone, R. William. *9/11 and the Future of Transportation Security*. Westport, CT: Praeger Security International, 2006.

Laville, Sandra, Richard Norton-Taylor, and Vikram Dodd. "A Plot to Commit Murder on an Unimaginable Scale." *Guardian*, August 11, 2006. Retrieved February 2008 (http://www.guardian.co.uk/uk/2006/aug/11/politics.usa1).

McLaughlin, Eliott C. "Federal ID Plan Raises Privacy Concerns." CNN, August 16, 2007. Retrieved February 2008 (http://www.cnn.com/2007/POLITICS/08/16/real.id/index.html).

National Commission on Terrorist Attacks Upon the United State (9/11 Commission). *The 9/11 Commission Report: The Final Report of the National Commission on Terrorists Attacks upon the United States. Authorized Edition*. New York, NY: W. W. Norton, 2004.

Providence Journal. "Extra: The Station Fire." 2008. Retrieved February 2008 (http://www.projo.com/extra/2003/stationfire).

Thomas, Andrew R. *Aviation Insecurity: The New Challenges of Air Travel*. Amherst, NY: Prometheus Books, 2003.

Thomas, R. Murray. *Violence in America's Schools: Understanding, Prevention, and Responses*. Westport, CN: Praeger, 2006.

Van Natta, Don, Jr., Elaine Sciolino, and Stephen Grey. "Details Emerge in British Terror Case." *New York Times*, August 26, 2006. Retrieved February 2008 (http://www.nytimes.com/2006/08/28/world/europe/28plot.html?ex=1314417600&en=3bd0e2092e48e4f1&ei=5090&partner=rssuserland&emc=rss).

Weil, Martin. "Gunman Shoots His Way into Capitol; Two Officers Killed, Suspect Captured." *Washington Post*, July 23, 1998. Retrieved February 2008 (http://www.washingtonpost.com/wp-srv/national/longterm/shooting/stories/main072598.htm).

Wilgoren, Jodi. "Tapes Show Desperation and Panic at Chicago Club's Exits." *New York Times*, March 1, 2003. Retrieved February 2008 (http://query.nytimes.com/gst/fullpage.html?res=9506E6D7103CF932A35750C0A9659C8B63).

Wilgoren, Jodi. "21 Die in Stampede of 1,500." *New York Times*, February 18, 2003. Retrieved February 2008 (http://query.nytimes.com/gst/fullpage.html?res=9A04E7D81F3AF93BA25751C0A9659C8B63).

Zeleny, Jeff, and Maria Newman. "Details of Omaha Shooting Emerge." *New York Times*, December 6, 2007. Retrieved February 2008 (http://www.nytimes.com/2007/12/06/us/06cnd-shoot.html).

Index

About the Author

Corona Brezina has written more than a dozen titles for Rosen Publishing. Several of her previous books have also focused on topics related to current events and social issues, including *Violence and Society: School and College Massacres* and *In the News: Climate Change.* She lives in Chicago.

Photo Credits

Cover (top, left) Omaha Police Department/Getty Images; cover (top, right) Chip Somodevilla/Getty Images; cover (bottom) Jed Jacobsohn/Getty Images; pp. 4, 13 Staff Sgt. Manuel J. Martinez/U.S. Air Force; pp. 5, 25 Tim Boyle/Getty Images; pp. 7, 22, 31, 33, 43, 48 © AP Images; p. 9 Scott Boehm/Getty Images; pp. 14, 20 Alex Wong/ Getty Images; p. 15 Joyce Naltchayan/AFP/Getty Images; p. 17 Luke Frazza/AFP/Getty Images; p. 23 Courtesy of Plymouth County Jail/Getty Images; p. 27 David Paul Morris/Getty Images; pp. 35, 38 CNN/Getty Images; p. 36 © Bob Daemmrich/AFP/Getty Images; pp. 47, 51 Dave Einsel/Getty Images; p. 54 Mario Tama/Getty Images.

Designer: Tom Forget; Photo Researcher: Amy Feinberg